INSPIRATIONAL LIVES

STEPHEN HAWKING

PIONEERING SCIENTIST

Sonya Newland

WAYLAND

First published in 2015 by Wayland

Copyright © Wayland 2015

Wayland
338 Euston Road
London NW1 3BH

Wayland Australia
Level 17/207 Kent Street
Sydney, NSW 2000

Produced for Wayland by
White-Thomson Publishing Ltd
www.wtpub.co.uk
+44 (0)843 208 7460

Design: Tim Mayer (Mayer Media)
Proofreader: Izzi Howell

A catalogue record for this title is
available from the British Library.

ISBN 978 0 7502 9014 2
ebook ISBN: 978 0 7502 9015 9

Dewey Number: 530.1'092-dc23

Printed in China

Wayland is a division of Hachette
Children's Books, an Hachette UK
company.

www.hachette.co.uk

Picture acknowledgements:
The author and publisher would like
to thank the following for allowing
their pictures to be reproduced in
this publication.
Alamy: 25 (NASA Collection); **Corbis:** 5
(Stuart Freedman/In Pictures), 24 (Andy
Rain/epa), 27 (Charles W. Luzier); **Getty
Images:** 14 (Gilles Bassignac), 17, 19, 20
(Roger Viollet); **NASA:** 4 (JPL-Caltech),
15 (CXC/M.Weiss), 18 (JPL-Caltech), 21
(X-ray: NASA/CXC/Stanford/J.Hlavacek-
Larrondo et al., Optical: NASA/ESA/
STScI/M.Postman & CLASH team), 22, 26;
Rex Features: 7, 9, 11, 12, 16 (Jason Bye),
28 (TM & copyright 20th Century Fox),
29 (Action Press); **Shutterstock:** 6 (Chris
Hill), 10 (Neil Mitchell), 13 (Featureflash);
Topfoto: 23 (UPP); **Wikimedia:** 8
(Gary Houston).

Contents

Black-hole breakthrough

One autumn day in 1973, Dr Stephen Hawking was in his office at Cambridge University doing calculations to find out more about black holes. It would have been a typical day at work, except that Stephen was puzzled by what the maths was telling him. He was sure his calculations were correct, but they turned upside down everything that scientists at the time believed about black holes.

Black holes are places in space where **gravity** is so strong that it pulls in everything around it. Even light cannot escape from a black hole. This is why we cannot see black holes – scientists only know they are there because of the way that other objects in space behave near them. So, if nothing could resist that super-strong gravity, why did Stephen's calculations show that particles and energy could stream back into space from a black hole?

The gravity in a black hole is so strong because matter has been squeezed down into a really small point. This can happen when a star collapses at the end of its long life.

WOW!

The largest black holes are called 'supermassive' and they have a mass more than one million times that of the Sun. The smallest black holes are the size of a single atom, but even these have the same mass as a mountain!

At first, Stephen didn't reveal his findings. He wanted to be absolutely sure that he was right. When he finally published his discovery the following year, it sent shockwaves through the physics community and made Stephen a scientific superstar. The energy that came out of black holes became known as 'Hawking radiation'.

Since the discovery of Hawking radiation, Stephen has made even more breakthroughs that have challenged scientists' understanding of the universe. He has also written several books that explain these difficult ideas in a way that everyone can understand. Amazingly, Stephen has achieved all this despite having a disease that means he cannot move or talk.

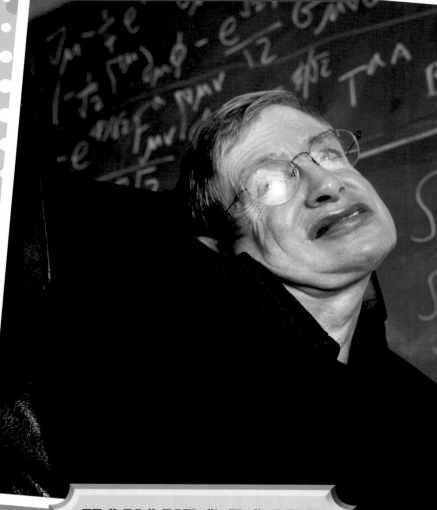

Today, Stephen Hawking is considered to be the most influential scientist since Albert Einstein.

HONOURS BOARD

Here are some of the awards Stephen has won for his work:

1975	Eddington Medal
1978	Albert Einstein Medal
1981	American Franklin Medal
1987	Paul Dirac Medal
2006	Copley Medal
2009	Presidential Medal of Freedom
2012	Fundamental Physics Prize

An eccentric childhood

Stephen Hawking was born in Oxford in 1942. This was at the height of the Second World War, and Stephen's family had moved to Oxford to escape the bombing in London. His parents, Frank and Isobel, had both studied at Oxford University so the city was a natural choice. In fact, Isobel was one of the first women to graduate from the university, at a time when few girls went on to higher education.

After the war, the Hawkings went back to London for a while, but when Stephen was eight they moved again – this time settling in a rickety three-storey house in St Albans. During this period the family grew, as Stephen was joined by two younger sisters, Mary and Philippa. When Stephen was 14, his parents also adopted another boy, Edward.

Galileo claimed that the planets moved around the Sun. This was a radical idea at the time, as most people in the sixteenth century believed that Earth was the centre of the universe.

GALILEO GALILEI

INSPIRATION

The day Stephen was born – 8 January 1942 – was the 300th anniversary of the death of the famous Italian physicist Galileo Galilei, whose improvements to the telescope helped people understand more about our **solar system**. As he grew older and came to love physics himself, Stephen was rather proud of this coincidence!

Stephen was close to both Philippa (in the middle) and Mary (on the right), even though Philippa was five years younger than him. He says that she was cleverer than him and he 'respected her opinions'.

Frank Hawking was a medical researcher who studied **tropical diseases**. He often travelled to Africa for work. Sometimes he took his wife and children with him, but more often Stephen and his sisters stayed at home with Isobel.

The whole family earned a reputation for being clever – and a bit **eccentric**! They all loved to read, and books were piled up all around the walls of the house. Often the whole family would sit around the dinner table eating in complete silence, each absorbed in a book.

WOW!

As children, Stephen and his sisters had a tendency to speak so quickly that they accidentally made up their own words. Friends and neighbours nicknamed this language 'Hawkingese'.

Frank drove around in an old black London taxi and kept bees in the cellar. He also enjoyed teaching his children how to make fireworks in the greenhouse!

Young Einstein

At school, Stephen showed few signs of the brilliance that he is now famous for. He always scored in the lower half of his class, and he demonstrated no particular talent for maths or science. Despite this, his friends knew he was clever. They nicknamed him 'Einstein', after the famous scientist who had come up with the **theories of relativity**.

WOW!

Stephen once won the **Divinity** Prize at school. At home, the Hawkings would often have debates about whether or not God exists. Stephen's work on the origins of the universe has led him to consider this question many times throughout his career.

Stephen's teachers also tried to bring out his full potential, but he was more interested in extra-curricular activities than schoolwork. He loved board games, and he and his friends would spend hours making up their own games with complicated rules.

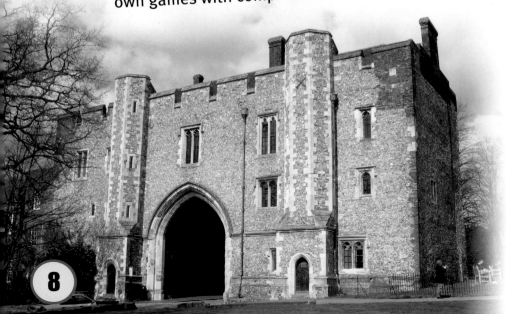

Stephen went to St Albans School (left). His father had wanted him to go to the well-known Westminster School, but Stephen was ill on the day he was meant to take the exam.

Stephen was fascinated by how things worked, and he enjoyed **dismantling** gadgets such as clocks and radios. He admits that he was not quite as good at putting them back together again! As a teenager, Stephen spent much of his free time building models of boats and planes. He says that he always aimed to 'build working models that I could control'.

In 1958, Stephen and his friends used parts from an old clock and a telephone switchboard to build a computer. They called it the 'Logical Uniselector Computing Engine' (LUCE) and it made the boys famous at school! The school newspaper reported that the computer could solve 'some useless though quite complex logical problems'. Sadly, this early example of Stephen's genius no longer exists – it was thrown away by accident after he left the school.

This is Stephen aged 12. Behind him is the ramshackle house he grew up in – his parents never got around to making all the repairs it needed!

TOP TIP

Stephen believes that a good scientist is always driven by a curiosity about how things work. His own obsession with taking things apart and building models was an early sign of this curiosity. 'Look up at the stars and not down at your feet,' he advises. 'Try to make sense of what you see. Wonder about what makes the universe exist.'

Studies at Oxford

Stephen's grades began to improve in his later years at school, but he was still little more than an average student. By the time he was 16 or 17, however, he had developed a real interest in maths and physics, and he began to consider studying these subjects at university.

INSPIRATION

Towards the end of his school career Stephen was greatly influenced by his maths teacher, Dikran Tahta. Dikran had helped the boys build LUCE and, recognizing Stephen's skill at maths, he encouraged the young man to study it at university. Dikran later became a respected mathematician and writer himself.

Although he refused to give in to his father's wishes and study medicine, Stephen *did* want to follow in his parents' footsteps and attend Oxford University. But the Hawkings were not a wealthy family and a university education was expensive. If he was going to continue his studies at all, Stephen really needed to win a **scholarship**.

Oxford University is one of the oldest and most famous universities in the world. It is also one of the hardest to get into!

Stephen impressed the tutors at Oxford when he went for his interview and, despite his low grades at school, he surprised everyone by acing the entrance exam. So, in October 1959, with a scholarship in physics, Stephen took his place at University College, Oxford.

To begin with, Stephen didn't enjoy university life. He got good marks, but he found his studies 'ridiculously easy' and he was both bored and lonely. This changed in his second year, when he began to take part in more of the social activities that were on offer. In particular, he loved being **cox** of the rowing team. He became a lively and popular student.

WOW!

Stephen estimates that he only spent an hour a day on his studies during his time at Oxford. Despite his lack of effort, he still graduated with a First Class degree!

Stephen (in the boat on the far right) would take the rowing team out in all weathers.

A devastating diagnosis

This is Stephen at his graduation from Oxford in 1962. That autumn he began his postgraduate degree at Trinity Hall, Cambridge.

In his last year at Oxford, Stephen began to notice some physical problems. He seemed to be getting clumsier and would often trip over. Sometimes his speech was slurred. However, these issues came and went, and he didn't see any reason to worry.

Stephen had more important things on his mind at the time – such as sitting his final exams and getting the marks he needed to do his **postgraduate** degree in **cosmology** at Cambridge University. His exam results were borderline, so he had to have an interview to decide on his final mark. He told his teachers that if they gave him a First he would go to Cambridge, but if they didn't he would stay at Oxford. They awarded him a First!

TOP TIP

Stephen's illness has taught him to think about the things he *can* do rather than the things he can't. His advice to others who have a disability is to 'concentrate on things your disability doesn't prevent you doing well … Don't be disabled in spirit.'

Stephen spent the summer of 1962 travelling with a friend, but he found the trip exhausting and he went off to Cambridge in October without feeling refreshed from the break. When he returned home for the Christmas holidays, his parents realized at once that something was wrong. He seemed to have lost his **coordination** – he could barely tie up his shoelaces – and he had difficulty speaking. Frank and Isobel made Stephen go to the doctor to find out what was wrong.

After several weeks of tests, doctors delivered the terrible news – Stephen had a disease called Amyotrophic Lateral Sclerosis, or ALS. This disease causes the nerves that control the body's muscles to slowly shut down. There is no cure for ALS and Stephen was given just two and a half years to live. He was 21 years old.

People diagnosed with ALS usually live for between two and five years. Stephen has beaten the odds and, 50 years on, he still leads an active life.

INSPIRATION

While he was still in hospital after being diagnosed with ALS, Stephen shared a room with a young man who had **leukaemia**. When he saw what his roommate went through, Stephen realized that there were people worse off than him, and he decided to make the most of what time he had left.

New lease of life

Naturally Stephen was devastated by the news. However, as he came to terms with the diagnosis, his attitude towards his studies changed dramatically. 'I was bored with life before my illness,' he later explained. 'There had not seemed to be anything worth doing.' Now, realizing that he had only a short time to achieve something worthwhile, he threw himself into his work.

Stephen and Jane got married in 1965. They had three children together – Robert, Lucy and Timothy.

Shortly before he found out about his ALS, Stephen had met a young woman called Jane Wilde at a party. Jane had been to the same school as Stephen, but they had not known each other well as children. On meeting again, they clearly enjoyed each other's company and Jane was a great help and support in the difficult early months after Stephen learnt of his illness.

WOW!

Stephen was interested in space from a young age. He would lie out under the stars with his mother and sisters and 'wonder where we came from'. Even when he was a child, Stephen says he wanted 'to fathom the far depths of the universe'.

Around the same time, Stephen met another mathematician and cosmologist working at Cambridge, Roger Penrose. Roger was studying a **phenomenon** called space-time singularities – places in the universe that go against the laws of physics. Stephen was enthralled by Penrose's ideas, and the two men began to work together.

Everything pulled into a black hole by the strength of its gravity is crushed into one single point – the singularity.

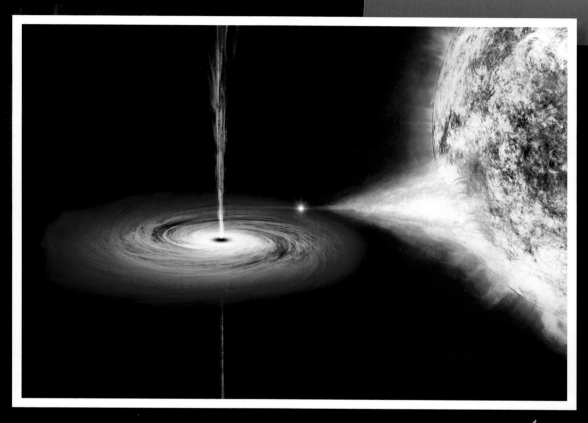

While his mind remained as active as ever, the disease continued to affect Stephen physically. By the early 1970s, he could no longer walk and had to use a wheelchair to get around. Despite this, his research was going well. In fact, he was on the brink of the discovery that would catapult him to fame.

INSPIRATION

Stephen met Roger Penrose while at Cambridge. Roger was ten years older than Stephen, and his ideas about black holes and singularities captured the younger man's imagination and interest. The two men carried out a lot of research together and **collaborated** on several writing projects, including the book *The Nature of Space and Time*.

A day in the life of Stephen Hawking

Stephen is now in his seventies. Most people have retired by the time they reach his age, but Stephen still goes to work every day. He explains that because of his disease, every day could be his last so he wants to 'make the most of every minute'.

For many years now, Stephen has had a full-time team of carers to assist him with his daily routine. Three assistants work in shifts to help with everything he needs, from getting out of bed to eating, working and communicating. Stephen has an office at Cambridge University, where he continues his research, advises students and prepares for **lectures** and interviews.

TOP TIP

To be a good theoretical physicist, you need to understand not only the latest scientific studies, but also what scientists believed in the past – and why. Read up on the history of ideas about the universe, such as the great debate over the **Steady State theory** and the **Big Bang theory** in the mid-twentieth century.

Stephen has help at work as well as at home. This picture shows him in his office with his personal assistant, his researcher and one of his carers.

It can take Stephen a while to instruct his computer with answers, so he is usually sent the list of questions a week or two before an interview takes place. He then types up and records the answers so that he can activate the recording during the interview. He follows the same process with his lectures – writing and recording them, then playing them back to lecture halls full of awed listeners.

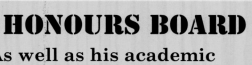

HONOURS BOARD

As well as his academic works, Stephen has written several books to explain complex science in a way that everyone can understand. These include:

1988 *A Brief History of Time*
1993 *Black Holes and Baby Universes and Other Essays*
2001 *The Universe in a Nutshell*
2002 *On the Shoulders of Giants*
2005 *A Briefer History of Time*
2005 *God Created the Integers*
2010 *The Grand Design*

Stephen is frequently invited to award ceremonies and other important events. In 2012, he gave a speech at the opening ceremony of the Paralympic Games in London.

Hawking radiation

In 1974, Stephen revealed to the world his theory that radiation could escape the gravity of a black hole. Other scientists were amazed. For years, they had believed that black holes were complete **vacuums**. Now someone was suggesting that they weren't.

Many experts didn't believe it could be true and they scrambled to carry out more research that would prove Stephen right or wrong. However, it wasn't long before Stephen's calculations convinced the scientific world. Soon, he was being showered with awards and honours. One of his proudest moments was when he was made a Fellow of the Royal Society – a special organization for brilliant scientists.

Cosmologists now believe that there is a supermassive black hole at the centre of every galaxy, including our galaxy, the Milky Way.

INSPIRATION

Stephen's childhood nickname, 'Einstein', proved to be a sign of what lay in his future. Albert Einstein's theories of relativity and space-time were the basis of much of Stephen's work during his early years as a cosmologist. Stephen later developed – and sometimes disagreed with! – Einstein's ideas.

In 1975, the Royal Astronomical Society awarded Stephen the famous Eddington Medal for his discovery. The same year, he travelled to Rome, where the Pope gave him the Pius XI Gold Medal – a special award for young scientists who show 'exceptional promise'.

In 1979, Stephen was made Lucasian Professor of Mathematics at Cambridge. In the past, this **prestigious** post has been held by famous figures including the physicist Sir Isaac Newton; the man who invented the computer, Charles Babbage; and the expert in **quantum physics** Paul Dirac. Stephen held the post for 30 years, stepping down in 2009.

WOW!
The post of Lucasian Professor of Mathematics at Cambridge University has only been held by 14 people since the position was created more than 350 years ago – in 1663. It is one of the greatest honours that a scientist can receive.

The second half of the 1970s passed in a whirlwind of travel as Stephen's fame spread. Here he is visiting Princeton University, in the United States, in October 1979.

A Brief History of Time

Being made Lucasian Professor was a high honour, but Stephen's career would soon reach even greater heights. He wanted everyone – not just scientists – to understand his fascination with space, so in the early 1980s he began working on a new book. However, before Stephen could finish it, he had to overcome more health problems.

TOP TIP

When writing his books, Stephen steers clear of scientific jargon. 'I was sure that nearly everyone is interested in how the universe operates,' he says, 'but most people cannot follow mathematical equations.' Instead he uses comparisons with everyday things to help people 'picture' the problem.

Stephen in his study in 1989. The photo in the middle of the bookshelf is of Albert Einstein!

Stephen's condition worsened and soon he needed round-the-clock care. By 1985, he could no longer speak. He started using a special computer program to talk.

Using this 'Equalizer' he could point to words on a computer screen, which were then turned into speech. At first Stephen could use his hands to point to the words. Today he controls the pointer using a sensor attached to one of his cheek muscles, because he cannot move any other part of his body.

During this period of illness Stephen had stopped work on his book. However, when he recovered he continued writing with enthusiasm and, with the help of this computer, he finally finished *A Brief History of Time*. It was published in 1988 and was an instant best-seller. It made Stephen a star!

For the first time, complicated questions about the **cosmos** were explained in a way that ordinary people could understand. How did the universe begin? Where and when might it end? What are black holes? How does gravity work? Stephen took his readers on a journey of discovery to reveal the mysteries of the universe.

A Brief History of Time *helped people understand how black holes were created, like the one at the centre of this galaxy cluster, 3.9 billion light years from Earth.*

HONOURS BOARD

A Brief History of Time has sold more than 10 million copies worldwide and has been translated into over 40 languages. It stayed on the *Times* best-seller list for 237 weeks!

Endings and beginnings

A *Brief History of Time* was enormously popular, but some people still found the science difficult. So, over the next few years Stephen wrote even more books that tried to make complex theories about the universe easy to understand. Stephen's research also continued during the 1980s and 1990s. One of the most important ideas that he came up with in this period was the 'no-boundaries' theory.

WOW!

When writing *A Brief History of Time*, Stephen was warned that for every equation he included, he would lose half his readers. In the end, he included only one equation – Einstein's famous $E=MC^2$!

For centuries, astronomers had tried to work out how *big* the universe was. Did it go on forever or – somewhere – was there an edge to it? In 1929, the **astronomer** Edwin Hubble discovered that the universe is actually expanding. This suggests that sometime in the far distant past, the universe was born and began to grow. It also suggests that the universe has an edge.

The Hubble Space Telescope, named after Edwin Hubble, allows scientists to see into deep space.

Stephen's no-boundaries theory claims that, in fact, there is no edge to the universe – a bit liked the curved surface of the Earth has no end. For a long time Stephen had been sure that there was something special about what scientists call the 'boundary conditions' of the universe. As he says, 'What can be more special than that there *is* no boundary?'

As Stephen concentrated on his writing and research, his marriage to Jane began to break down. In particular, his work on the origins of the universe had led him to the conclusion that God did not exist – a belief that upset Jane deeply. At the same time, Stephen had grown close to Elaine Mason, one of his nurses. In 1995, Stephen and Jane were divorced, and Stephen married Elaine.

Stephen explained his no-boundaries theory in his 2001 book The Universe in a Nutshell.

WOW!

If the no-boundaries theory is correct, time did not exist before the Big Bang. This is hard to imagine, but think about travelling to the South Pole. When you get there, you can't go any further south. There is no *physical* boundary – it's simply the point where 'south' ends. If you travelled back to the beginning of the universe, this would be where time ends (or begins)!

Theories of everything

Over the years, scientists have come up with many theories about how the universe was created and the laws of physics that control it. Some deal with forces such as gravity, which affects huge things like planets. Others explain the forces that act on tiny particles in the **nucleus** of an atom. But so far, no one has come up with a theory that explains *everything* – the very large and the very small.

WOW!

Most people experience the world in four dimensions: three dimensions of space (width, height and length) and one of time. Stephen's amazing mathematical mind allows him to think about things in 11 dimensions, he says!

Stephen applies his genius to earthly matters as well as the mysteries of space. In 2014, he developed a formula for how England could win the World Cup!

The idea that there might be a single 'unifying theory' has obsessed scientists for nearly 100 years. Like many others, Stephen has spent much of his career trying to figure it out. In *A Brief History of Time*, he explained that finding it would be 'the ultimate triumph of human reason'. His search for this 'answer to everything' has even led him to believe that it might be possible to travel through time!

By the start of the twenty-first century, Stephen was widely believed to be the greatest living scientist. He continued to write and to travel all over the world, and was recognized wherever he went. During a lecture in Israel, he joked about his fame: 'It is not enough for me to wear dark sunglasses and a wig. The wheelchair gives me away!'

As well as writing more accessible science books for adults, Stephen also wanted to share his extraordinary ideas with a younger audience. So, with his daughter Lucy, he began work on a series of fiction books for children. These narrate the adventures of a boy called George and the world's most powerful computer, Cosmos. Together they uncover the mysteries of the universe.

HONOURS BOARD

Stephen's books for children include:

2007 *George's Secret Key to the Universe*

2009 *George's Cosmic Treasure Hunt*

2011 *George and the Big Bang*

2014 *George and the Unbreakable Code*

In 2008, after their first George book was published, Stephen and Lucy Hawking shared the stage for a series of lectures organized by NASA.

Space traveller

Having studied the mysteries of the universe his whole life, Stephen has always wanted to go into space himself. This is something that most able-bodied space enthusiasts can only dream about, but for someone like Stephen who can't move at all, it seemed an unlikely **ambition**.

Before Stephen was awarded the famous Copley Medal for scientific achievement in 2006, NASA astronauts took his medal into space – along with a photo of him!

However, in 2007 Stephen was thrilled to discover what it would feel like to really go into space. He was invited to the Kennedy Space Center in Florida, USA. To help astronauts train for their journey to space, the KSC has special planes. These have been nicknamed 'vomit comets' because the feeling of being in zero gravity often makes people sick the first time they try it! Stephen was specially invited by NASA to have a go in one of these.

TOP TIP

To be a good scientist, you need to be prepared to make mistakes and to find out that your ideas are wrong – but keep trying anyway. This is the only way that science can advance and develop. Stephen says that mistakes are 'a good thing ... without imperfection, neither you nor I would exist.'

Stephen found the whole day amazing. As the plane soared over the Atlantic Ocean, he felt what it was like to be out of his wheelchair for the first time in years. He didn't want the experience to end. 'I could have gone on and on,' he said. 'Space, here I come!' Having had this practice, he hopes that one day he really will get to travel into space.

WOW!

Stephen believes that humans will not survive another thousand years unless we settle on other planets. 'There are too many accidents that can befall life on a single planet,' he explains.

Stephen sets off for the Zero-G plane that turned him into an astronaut for a day.

The impact of Stephen Hawking

Stephen has challenged accepted scientific beliefs and forced experts to think about the laws of physics in different ways. But it is not just other scientists that Stephen has **enlightened** and educated. He has also broadened the public's understanding of the universe – its past, its present and what may lie in its future.

Everyone has heard of Stephen. He is so well-known that he has been invited to appear on many popular TV shows and comedies, including *The Simpsons*, *Futurama*, *Star Trek: The Next Generation* and *The Big Bang Theory*.

WOW!

Stephen came up with his latest theories about black holes while trying to solve a puzzle called the 'black hole firewall paradox'. This tries to work out what would happen to an astronaut who was pulled into a black hole!

Stephen's appearances on shows like *Futurama* prove he has a great sense of humour alongside his brilliant mind!

His own story has also been dramatized several times, including the 2014 film *Theories of Everything*, which stars Eddie Redmayne as Stephen and which tells the story of his relationship with his first wife, Jane. Stephen himself returned to more serious science programmes in 2014, with a series called *Stephen Hawking's Science of the Future*. This looks at some of the most recent scientific breakthroughs that might soon change our world.

Stephen is still coming up with radical new theories of his own. He recently suggested that black holes do not exist in the way he had thought back when he discovered Hawking radiation. This constant challenging of ideas (sometimes his own!) is what science – and life – is all about for Stephen. He describes himself as 'a child that has never grown up' and says he always asks these 'how and why questions'. Who knows what amazing discoveries his curiosity may lead to in the future?

Stephen shows no signs of scaling back his busy schedule of travelling, writing and lecturing. He wants to live every day as if it were his last.

HONOURS BOARD

As well as writing books, Stephen has been involved in several documentary films and television programmes, including:

1992 *A Brief History of Time*
1997 *Stephen Hawking's Universe*
2008 *Stephen Hawking: Master of the Universe*
2010 *Into the Universe with Stephen Hawking*
2011 *Brave New World with Stephen Hawking*
2012 *Stephen Hawking's Grand Design*
2013 *Hawking*

Have you got what it takes to be a pioneering scientist?

1 Do you look up at the night sky and wonder about the stars and planets – what they're made of, how far away they are and what lies beyond them?
a) I'm fascinated by space and love finding out what scientists know about the universe.
b) I find the stars and planets interesting, but some of the science is hard to understand!
c) I'm more interested in what's happening on planet Earth.

2 Do you enjoy studying science and maths at school?
a) Science is my favourite subject, especially physics, and I'm also good at maths.
b) I enjoy science and maths and am pretty good at them, although I sometimes find them difficult.
c) I'm better at arts or languages than I am at science and maths.

3 Are you good at explaining scientific ideas in a simple way?
a) I have a knack for describing difficult ideas in a way that other people find easy to understand.
b) I can find the right words most of the time.
c) I have trouble understanding science myself, so I don't think I could explain it to someone else!

4 Can you come up with new ways of thinking about things and then put your ideas into action?
a) I'm a leader not a follower, and I often have ideas that no one else has thought of.
b) I can come up with new ideas if I'm pointed in the right direction.
c) I prefer to be told what to do.

5 Do you approach problems logically?
a) I love puzzles and problems and I always take a logical, organized approach to solving them.
b) I'm pretty logical, but it sometimes takes me a while to work out the best way to solve a problem.
c) I'm a bit scatty and I give up easily if I don't understand something.

6 Do you have the patience and determination to keep searching for answers, even if it might take years to find them?
a) 'If at first you don't succeed, try and try again' is my motto.
b) I'll keep going for a while, but I'll give up eventually if it seems hopeless.
c) I prefer quick results and I get disheartened if I find out I'm wrong.

RESULTS

Mostly As: It sounds as if you have the right attitude and abilities to be a good scientist. Make sure you keep up your studies and follow the latest ideas about the workings of the universe.

Mostly Bs: You have the potential to be a good scientist, but you might need to focus more on your maths and science and learn to be a bit more patient if you don't find the answers right away!

Mostly Cs: You probably aren't cut out for a life of study and research, but you might still want to get out and enjoy the wonders of the night sky every now and then.

Glossary

ambition A goal that someone really wants to achieve in their life.

astronomer A scientist who studies space and the things in it, such as planets and stars.

atom The smallest part of a chemical element.

Big Bang theory A theory about the universe which says that it began as a single point about 14 billion years ago and has been expanding ever since.

collaborated Worked together.

coordination The ability to use different parts of your body smoothly at the same time.

cosmology The scientific study of the origins of the universe.

cosmos The universe as an orderly system, where everything works in harmony.

cox The member of a rowing team who steers the boat and coordinates the rhythm of the rowers.

dismantling Taking apart.

divinity The study of religion.

eccentric Unusual and a bit strange.

enlighten To make someone aware of or help them to understand something.

fathom To work something out so you understand it fully.

gravity A natural force that attracts two objects together.

lectures Long speeches on a particular topic, usually intended to be educational.

leukaemia Cancer of the blood.

mass The amount of matter, or 'stuff', in an object.

nucleus The central part of an atom, which contains the particles called protons and neutrons.

phenomenon Something amazing or unusual.

postgraduate A second degree that someone can take after they have done an undergraduate degree.

prestigious Something that is important and highly regarded.

quantum physics The scientific study of the tiny particles that exist within atoms.

scholarship A financial reward given to students for academic achievement, to help them further their education.

solar system A group of planets and the star that they revolve around. Our solar system consists of eight planets (including Earth) and the Sun.

Steady State theory A theory about the universe which says that it has stayed the same throughout time and that it has no beginning or end.

theories of relativity Theories developed by Albert Einstein which state that the way everything (except light) moves through time and space depends on the position and movement of the person watching it.

tropical diseases Diseases that are usually found in the hottest parts of the world.

vacuums Areas that have no matter in them at all – not even air.

Index

INSPIRATIONAL LIVES

Contents of new titles in the series

David Attenborough
978 0 7502 8569 8

Life in the wild
The Attenborough boys
Wartime studies
Breaking into television
Animal encounters
In charge at the BBC
A day in the life of David Attenborough
Life on Earth
Knight of the realm
From Antarctica to paradise
The end of *Life*
Life in 3D
The impact of David Attenborough
Have you got what it takes to be a naturalist?

Tim Berners-Lee
978 0 7502 9012 8

'This is for everyone'
Cardboard computer
A banana skins itself
Whistling trains
Do it yourself
Stepping into the world
A day in the life
Enquire within upon everything
Two proposals
The first website
Going global
The Consortium
A world wide change
Have you got what it takes to be an inventor?

Stephen Hawking
978 0 7502 9014 2

Black-hole breakthrough
An eccentric childhood
Young Einstein
Studies at Oxford
A devastating diagnosis
New lease of life
A day in the life of Stephen Hawking
Hawking radiation
A Brief History of Time
Endings and beginnings
Theories of everything
Space traveller
The impact of Stephen Hawking
Have you got what it takes to be a pioneering scientist?

Malala Yousafzai
978 0 7502 8464 6

'Who is Malala?'
The birth of a girl
Selling books for sweets
Kites and classrooms
A great earthquake
Radio Mullah
A day in the life
Escape from Mingora
Death threats
The shooting
'Father' and 'country'
Back to school
'I am Malala'
Have you got what it takes to be an activist?

WAYLAND